WAY MORE THAN LUCK

WAY MORE THAN LUCK
Ben Wilkinson

Seren is the book imprint of
Poetry Wales Press Ltd.
57 Nolton Street, Bridgend, Wales, CF31 3AE
www.serenbooks.com
facebook.com/SerenBooks
twitter@SerenBooks

The right of Ben Wilkinson to be identified as
the author of this work has been asserted in accordance
with the Copyright, Designs and Patents Act, 1988.

© Ben Wilkinson, 2018

ISBN: 978-1-78172-425-5
ebook: 978-1-78172-426-2
Kindle: 978-1-78172-427-9

A CIP record for this title is available from the British Library.

The publisher acknowledges the financial assistance of the Welsh Books Council.

Printed by Airdire Print Services Ltd.

Contents

III. *An Absurd Pastime*

I

Way More Than Luck

Depression is a kind of quantum physics of thought and emotion. It reveals what is normally hidden ... it is still more characterised by what we don't know than what we do. It is 90 per cent mystery.

Matt Haig,
Reasons to Stay Alive

I've learned that finishing a marathon isn't just an athletic achievement. It is a state of mind; a state of mind that says anything is possible.

John Hanc,
The Essential Runner

The Catch

For you, the catch wasn't something caught –
not word or contender, attention or fire.
Not the almost-missed train, or the sort
of wave surfers might wait an entire
lifetime for. Not the promise that leaves
the old man adrift for days, his boat
creaking, miles offshore. Nor what cleaves
the heart in two, that left your throat
parched and mute for taking pill
after yellow-green pill, the black-blue
taste the price you paid to kill
the two-parts sadness to one-part anger.
No. The catch was what you could never
let go. It's what you carried, and still do.

To David Foster Wallace

Since I was old enough to know myself
I've been trying to figure it out –
the constant gnawing sense of having
had and lost some infinite thing,
like half the time I'd chuck it all in;
throw the whole lot for a song.

I've been thinking it over again,
but more than that – it's always there
though you can dupe yourself into
thinking it's not, but *dupe* is wrong:
it's good as gone just so long
as I keep on, know that it's waiting.

You know what I mean. You know
like you knew what everyone with an ounce
of self-reflection feels or will feel,
can't put into words – my chest
bumps like a dryer with shoes in it.
I feel despair. The word's overused

and banalified now, despair,
but it's a serious word and we're using it
seriously. It's not desiring the fall;
it's fearing the flames. It takes
great personal courage to appear weak.
We all worship some hidden belief.

Here's mine: that if I prove enough
to myself I might stop and think
deep down, I'm not a piece of shit.
Get it? No punchline, just this sick
inertia turning in the stomach,
like the moment before

the accident happens, stretched out
indefinitely. Diluted panic:
dissolve one part into five parts
excuse for a human being.
Brief interviews with hopeless men.
That's shit: I can't make you

feel what I felt. So I try again –
stuck after work in some queue,
like you, like all of us going about
the tedium that strings our lives
together: paperchain people,
baskets lined under strip-lights.

Zone out the muzak. Focus. Try
to ease the unpindownable feeling
of hopelessness, hard frustration:
choose to see this moment
as radiant within the cosmos,
or bring another interpretation.

We're all utterly alone, but we're
utterly alone in this together.
Total and particulate as weather,
this queue shares its riffs
on all our dreams and nightmares
with each other, though all of us

wait for something to happen
as if we aren't part of it, hurrying
on to somewhere else. David,
days I'm up to here with this bullshit.
I know I'm not the only one.
You're long gone, and anyway

no prophet. No one can grant us
the will, patience or grace to go on;
least of all the self-loathing, cut-up
fool I've become, or always was.
Time waits for no man –
a platitude you'd have ridiculed

only to then prove true. Time,
as the poet said, licks its steady way
through stone – though it can stand
still, if you really want it to.
To which: if you buy that, you'll buy
anything. But I remember

running pure gradient in wind and rain,
my breath dogged on the fellside
only to round a corner into a peace
I'd never known awake: just the sound
of my bolting heartbeat, as rippled
sunlight carried across the tarn. I go

back to that time and again, when the
listless dark starts to creep in. But I sound
like I'm preaching, and that's not what
I meant – your smarts always came
without the pious crap. You never know
when it's coming, and that's the kicker

alright. Someone once called you
the voice of your generation; I'll buy that,
even though you'd shrug it off. This is all
we've got. I hit my thirties still hoping
against hope I can turn meagre words
into actions. Wish me way more than luck.

Days

when you weren't anyone. Days gone undercover.
Days half-dead in half-light, days under the covers.

Days hoping for a dawn that wouldn't come, days nights
and the sun a dull, faded thing seen through nights

of curtains drawn through days of nothing but you, you
being the last thing you'd want to think about, you

being, you'd discovered, precisely the fucking problem.
Days indistinguishable. Everything a problem.

Days gone, days not done but done-in from the start,
days of never touching a pen or making a start

but thoughts a blank: days of feeling nothing
then everything, everything come to nothing.

Days put behind you. Days that don't deserve the name.
Days put behind you. Days would never be the same.

Sundays too my Dad got up early

though no one knows where he went.
While Mum dozed in bed
and my brother and I watched
cartoons on the crackling set,

I like to think he built a secret
passion for distance running,
swift feet leaving the estate
in Ron Hill shorts and vest,
a cool breeze nipping at his neck.

While we ate up Looney Tunes
and Mum fussed in the kitchen,
he'd be halfway to Milford,
deftly dancing over tree roots,
trails in the cold morning light.

Then I'd know why I lace up
before the day's begun
in slate rain and deepest dark,
to get gone before anyone
can hold me back.

Where I Run From

after a line from Haruki Murakami

What I talk about when I talk about running
is nothing. Running is not a keep-fit regime –
your limits are not your limits. Running is not
escapism – the miles hammer back to the heart.
Running is not the tough guy's stance. It's you
versus you, the you *you* used to be, before you
realised pain is certain, but sorrow is a choice.
Running is not opposition, though it can be
competitive as camaraderie, the respect
that comes with knowing all that went into it:
the discipline. The work. The setbacks. The self.
Running is the pure solitude of a wordless hour.
What I talk about when I talk about running
is nothing. Talk is talk. Running is being.

Nesh

Not cold but given to feeling the cold,
a slip of a boy waiting
for the number 12
as a summer breeze floats in,
suddenly shivering. Or the way

my mum used to tell my brother
and me to take our coats off
even though we'd soon be out again:
"You'll not feel the benefit!" she'd scold,
sagely, and who were we to argue?

Nesh is for those of us who sense
someone walking over our grave,
who need the perfect
imprecision of the poem, made
from language's shoddy array,

to get us through the day.
Look at you, sat on the doorstep
having forgotten your keys again,
the slightest chill biting
at your neck. I'd give you my coat

if you weren't fifteen years dead.

'Pal'

Old familiar, the one who's friend and foe.
Knowing it's been too long since last time
he's come again, especially to see you.
Wants to hear how you've been: *fine, fine,*
can't complain, things are pretty good y'know,
great actually… and he listens in close
as you talk, smiles his smile. The all-time low.
He leaves the way the worm leaves the rose.
Next time you're trying to stand your ground –
argue your case, sprint the home straight,
stare yourself down in the mirror at eight –
he'll be there alright. His smile is a frown.
His frown is a scowl. His scowl is the fear
you hoped was long gone. Still here. Still here.

Some Relief

Relief as the sunset's small reprieve; relief as the look on
the found boy's sorry face; relief in pissing in the woods
on a freezing winter hike; relief as belch or burp; relief as
the train doors still open; relief when slowly sinking into
the bath's warm curve; relief in a filing cupboard; relief
waking to the panic of Monday morning moments before
the dawning revelation of Sunday; relief as laughter in
the company of strangers; relief as laughter at one's own
absurdity; relief in the dog's eyes, thundering downstairs
to find you home from the shops; relief as waived cost;
relief as light strained through the bars of a prison cell,
your prison cell, on the day of release; relief in a kindly
face; relief in an act of kindness, given or received, amid
the city's faceless stream; relief at the kind of day that
makes the rest of this life worthwhile; relief in coming
down; relief in standing on the fell after rainfall, looking
down at the town, the houses, your house, smaller than
you imagined, everything somehow more manageable
for now.

You / *You*

I'm just relaying what the voice in my head's saying
— Eminem, 'The Monster'

You trying to be the right guy   *Yeah right. Nice try*
You hating yourself and wanting out   *Washout*
You looking to prove something   *Go swing*
You wanting maybe praise or congrats   *Fuck that*
You hating any praising   *Look what it's written in*
You starting again, keeping it at bay   *Kiddin' me?*
You knowing it knows you like you do   *Too true*
You laughing like it was never here   *Fair's fair*
You hearing the silence under the quiet   *Keep it shut*
You waiting on… can't say what   *Worth a shot*
You not having the nerve   *Get what you deserve*
You trying to… what. 'Man up'?   *Useless fuck*
You working just to mess things up   *Yup*
You failing on its only terms   *You'll learn*

Graft

It must get easier over time though
he smiles, guessing
drills in the blistering cold,
running full tilt

can't be as hard as it sounds,
mile after mile
climbing the old hill
of weakness versus the will

else how do you do it?
Again, the sorry hope
that it might come simply
shows its idle head,

or worse, attempts
to dismiss its own failure
as the luck, chance
or dumb skill of the best.

We're all guilty of it.
No wonder in a world
where wealth is laid
for some on a gilded plate.

But anything worthwhile
is pure heart and courage.
I'm not talking the rich
and their inheritance.

Fuck that shit. Graft hard,
and hold true to this –
no one got anywhere fast
without striving for it.

Hound

When it comes, and I know how it comes
from nowhere, out of night
like a shadow falling on streets,
how it waits by the door in silence –
a single black thought, its empty face –

don't let it tie you down to the house,
don't let it slope upstairs to spend
hours coiled next to your bed,
but force the thing out, make it trudge
for miles in cold and wind and sleet.

Have it follow you, the faithful pet
it pretends to be, this mutt
like a poor-man's Cerberus,
tell it where to get off when it hangs
on with its coaxing look,

leave it tethered to a lamppost
and forget those pangs of guilt.
Know it's no dog but a phantom,
fur so dark it gives back nothing,
see your hand pass through

its come-and-go presence,
air of self-satisfied deception,
just as the future bursts in on
the present, its big *I am*, and that
sulking hound goes to ground again.

Running through Woods
on Bonfire Night

Racing this wood's pathways
one cold November night
the sky blooms green, a blaze
that pulls the darkness tight

this cold November night
you're running through the dark
fire's work, the dark so tight
the snare drum of your heart

is the backbeat to the dark
a field's song of burning
the snare drum of your heart
and you're still running, running

in a field's song of burning
chasing this wood's pathways
and you're still running, running
the sky burns red, ablaze

The Nightmare

Remember that long drive back from the Lakes,
lightning-lit through endless rain?
Nights I dream us on that stretch again,
the road a river with a line of silver
that leaps about its centre;
leading us to Newby, Lawkland, Cleatop.

These times, though, the car shudders
like someone about to vomit —
a thunderbolt, throwing
us forward through time
with the dashboard dials spinning;
making a DeLorean out of your Yaris.

The windscreen warps with scenery,
a zoetrope at full tilt.
We watch the road narrow
into a dirt track, cars evaporate,
trees shrivel into nothing
while others burst up in their place.

Dumbstruck, we sit in its wake.
And I want to tell you the world
we find is a glorious one,
paradise pooled in light,
but I can't. Stepping
into heat, a murder of crows

scatters in the field to the west;
the trees diagrams of harm,
the earth barren in a stony calm.
Walking, silence for what seems
like hours. Then, when I turn to say
as much, you're nowhere to be found.

The nightmare should end there.
Instead I carry on, hopelessly
trekking a dust trail. All to find
nothing apart from that outline
in the heat, a shape
on the horizon. It's then I wake.

The River Don

                    rushes by, a current pushing on
past rows of fig trees blooming from its banks
and factory outfalls, spilling nearby.
Remember how the floods two years back
rose to the mark on The Fat Cat's wall –
that third summer of ours when the rain did
nothing but pour, the thought of what we might
wake to that dream of mine, the same dream
on/off for weeks?
                    It never reached us. We didn't
climb downstairs half-asleep to find our furniture
floating, or ornaments, CDs and kept cassette tapes
making their bids to escape. Instead, the house
sat safe and sound: floors dry, photo frames still,
something else edging closer, the way water will.

II

An Ordinary Game

At the end of the storm / there's a golden sky / and the sweet silver song of the lark ...
'You'll Never Walk Alone'

What a great day for football. All we need is some green grass and a ball.

Bill Shankly,
manager of Liverpool Football Club 1959–1974

This one's for the kids stood on each other's shoulders
edging for a glimpse of their latest hero at Melwood;

for the single dad and his redoubtable daughter,
huddled together for what's unsaid yet understood;

for the blood of lads at trials who'll never make it,
taste the bittersweet thrill of pulling the shirt on once;

for the strange hope, indefatigable in replica kit,
a name to conjure with, court the gods of chance;

for what it means to shiver in February rain
on a Monday night, carrying home that 2-0 loss;

and to do the same next week, next month, again
weighing the distance run against its cost.

This is for a love beyond the smear campaigns,
the media's hooligans. This is for the beautiful game.

Bill Shankly

Always pass the ball forward, lads. Always pass
to a red shirt. A football team's like a piano.
You need eight to carry it, and three who can
play the damn thing. Ours is a simple sport:
the give and take of passes, control of the ball.
Make yourself available. It is that simple.
Thing is, some know the rules, but they don't know
the game. Lads, you'll do well if you remember
two things: believe that you're the best, and then
make sure of it. At a club, there's a holy trinity:
the players, the manager and the supporters.
Football is not a matter of life and death.
It is much more important than that. The trouble
with you, son, is that all your brains are in your head.

This is Anfield

Living up to its fabled buzz, the Kop roared and rose
even before kick-off. Down in the main stand
I watched; John Barnes adjusting his captain's band
on the flawless turf Waves of red in rows
and rows – a kid in that season's kit, I grinned
with a kind of borrowed pride, belonging
without belonging; my dad and brother craning
to see McManaman darting, how Fowler ignited
strike after strike.
             Half-time over, and a flying header
left the keeper without a chance... the place erupted.
I still remember it like that: the luminous pitch,
echo of the terraces, players floodlit
beneath an October sky. An ordinary game,
solid win, save for one kid looking on in wonder.

John Barnes

'Those people couldn't get under my skin.'

Brazil boasted Pelé, Garrincha and Zico
but drooled the day an English lad skipped
past their back five, a dancing shadow
striking home to leave the hosts speechless,
the National Front quiet. Years later,
a Merseyside tie at Goodison –
dark slurs circle the stands as malice
gets hurled over touchlines, head hung
as you back-heel (of all things) a banana,
launched by some half-cut thug. Play on.
And you would –
                             hurtling up the wing
to arch a sweeping, goal-bound ball,
the Blues slumped amid a Kopite song:
He stands proud, while all defenders fall.

Bruce Grobbelaar

(i)

So the story goes, Bruce is in the dressing room –
his teammates, opposition, the officials
and tens of thousands waiting on him and him alone.
He has to flick the lights out by kicking
the ball from the other side of the room, else
no clean sheet, no win, no theatrical penalty save.
The referee comes in, cops a volley in the face.

(ii)

What have Bruce Grobbelaar and an arsonist
got in common? They both throw matches.
I saw Bruce Grobbelaar outside Toys 'R' Us
the other day. He was giving away games.
So the story goes. Faced with a keeper wobbling
his legs in mock fear, the striker balloons
the ball into the crowds. Thus the cup is won.

Billy Liddell

This coal mining father set on better
for his son, digs deep to fork out for boots
in a family fed on porridge, hard slog.
Head down, he gets on: model sportsman
who plays it fast and hard but impeccably fair.
Give it to Billy! sears through the stands,
a boy who lobs them something to sing
about in the lean years of the second tier.

They don't make 'em like that anymore
almost too good to be true, the loyal hero
who married football with war, never
touched a drop, could head the ball home
from outside the box. *Liddellpool.* Listen
close. No wonder the stands still sound with it.

Steven Gerrard

Schoolkid knocking the ball to the bus-stop
from Melwood, years' work till the call-up
one grim winter night: yours is the real grit
the diehard fans can't help but prize.

A local lad done good. Skittish with nerves,
that fraught season on and under the wing
of your boyhood club. Then you, stepping up –
ten years a legend and the graft of games

seized by scruffs of necks, each win fought for.
Earned. *We go again. Don't let this fuckin' slip...*
That distant prize, almost within reach.

But no one predicts fate's last-ditch twist.
You, the one-club man striving tirelessly;
as if, with belief, we might achieve anything.

Robbie Fowler

Heard

the   one   about   the

lad   from   Toxteth   who

became

God?

Fernando Torres

A latter-day Daedalus, Benítez
sailed him from Atlético, crafted wings
which saw him twist and drift and float.

From the first inch-perfect shot tearing
Chelsea wide apart; that blissful sting
hitting home in the hush of Old Trafford;

to the chest, touch and volley on the turn
in the brief and fabled heat of '08,
he set the crowd alight. But he flew

too close. Goals dried up, and true
to the craftsman ruing his handiwork,
Rafa saw that formation fall apart.

He left a broken man, as *El Niño* would too –
lone pilot, drowned in money and talk.

The Kop

*'An anthropologist studying this Kop crowd would be introduced into
a rich and mystifying popular culture. They seem, mysteriously, to be
in touch with one another...'*
　　　　　　　　　　– BBC correspondent, reporting from the Spion Kop
　　　　　　　　　　stand at Anfield, home of Liverpool Football Club, 1964

Who remembers this singing, swaying mass
stood loud on the boards fifty years back?

A sounding board that's a single voice,
rhythms tuned to the game's dark pulse

from blizzard footage of Shankly's men
to the here-and-now and back again.

Find yourself here and you'll lose yourself

deep in the words yelled from without
now within, and again, again, every doubt

now a hope, each prayer a kid's wish,
the twelfth man darting about this pitch

with songs of old and songs sung anew.
Keep faith. Sing proud, sing red and true.

Lose yourself here, and you find yourself

Dreams and Songs to Sing

all round the fields of Anfield Road
round the fields of Anfield Road all
the fields of Anfield Road all round
fields of Anfield Road all round the
of Anfield Road all round the fields
Anfield Road all round the fields of
Road all round the fields of Anfield
all round the fields of Anfield Road
Road Anfield of fields the round all
Anfield of fields the round all Road
of fields the round all Road Anfield
fields the round all Road Anfield of
the round all Road Anfield of fields
round all Road Anfield of fields the
all Road Anfield of fields the round
Road Anfield of fields the round all

Luis Suárez

*'I cannot stand to miss even a single ball
because that might cost me everything.'*

Watch him pull the ball out of the sky   long pass
          fated for nothing   made into glory
     control   chip   control   side-step   strike
        blink-and-you'll-miss-it   or that impossible
free kick   keeper and wall   perfectly positioned
     still he finds   that postage-stamp-inch of space
        or this halfway-line lob   twist through air
such casual grace   poise   watch with disbelief
     watch it and square it with   the defender's horror
        as he starts to watch teeth   sink into flesh
        back to that   unstoppable kid for whom
          the game   was never   *just a game*
       the youth referee   cradles   his bloodied face
     rush of blood to the head   without which

Brother Football

for Sam

You're the bicycle kick in extra time
every time you enter a room:

back of the net or ballooned
into the stands. Pumped up

with a tough exterior, you're subtler
than you let on, the dummy

or nutmeg that sees you caught, mid-
action, centre stage for the frantic

ninety minutes. But I remember you
with the fondness of kickabouts,

rough and ready as jumpers for goalposts,
the pair of us stood in the week-long rain

of the long summer holidays.
Deflated, weathered, all but done,

you always picked yourself up.
You always played on.

Kenny Dalglish

Day breaks to heavy clouds over Anfield Road,
the Sabbath beyond that echoing afternoon.
Gates opened, the faithful bring flowers,
wreaths, notes… sisters, mothers, fathers
weeping, placing them in the goalmouth,
the eighteen-yard box, past the halfway line.
You'd think for all the world it'd snowed.
Then one man, making no fuss, steps up,
sits down two teddy bears, gifted by his kids;
a man who's performed miracles on this field,
resurrected hopes. Who'll pay his respects
to every one, not in duty's name, but love's.
They supported Liverpool Football Club.
It's the turn of the Club to support them.

III

An Absurd Pastime

What passes for hip cynical transcendence of sentiment is really some kind of fear of being really human, since to be really human... is probably to be unavoidably sentimental and naïve and goo-prone and generally pathetic.

David Foster Wallace,
Infinite Jest

You live and learn. At any rate, you live.

Douglas Adams,
Mostly Harmless

An Absurd Pastime

We spend our years trying to get it right,
sit sleepless when it wakes us in the night.

We're hoarding up its borrowed time again,
but now is never quite the same as then.

Practise makes perfect: can't argue with it.
It's easier to keep on than to quit.

It eats up every minute of every day.
We all know what it is I'm trying to say.

You Must Be Joking

What makes you want to get up in front
of a room, just so people can fall apart
laughing at you? I've asked myself
that question more times than I've sat

in my car at two, shivering and eating
a beige Cornish pasty, ticking over
before some godforsaken motorway
service station. Here it comes again:

the bellyache of a theatre doubled over,
punchline of some off-the-peg number,
a tall story with just enough familiarity
to hold a strange, comforting mirror

to the dead end of the working week.
If not truth exactly, what I speak
is that part of everyone they thought
was 'just them', or else plain shits

and giggles. Give in. Feel the warm glow
of laughter; laughing so hard you cry
in a room sick with laughter; laughing
till you can't. Now we're getting somewhere.

Building A Brighter, More Secure Future

Conservative Party election manifesto slogan, 2015

You must understand what we are building
is not the housing we promised. Not a
hospital, or school. It is a brighter
notion, an idea of Britain, where more
food banks will flourish, but for those secure
there is no cause for alarm. The future

is a place where the rich hand the future
to the poor, in which the great buildings
of Canary Wharf, climbing secure
above Tower Hamlets, offer up a
glut of wealth to the unfortunate, more
than you can imagine. This is a brighter

future, we promise, it is much brighter
than a concept like equality. A future
cannot be built on that. We all want more,
and some people are better at building
wealth, or else inheriting it, so a
tax for those who are beyond secure

is unfair: they made their money secure
through society, and being brighter –
or otherwise having been born to a
fortune – will make sure that in the future
sometime, this trickles down. As a building
stands firm, you have our word that more

will come to those without. Making more
is paramount to our concerns. To secure
this, in the meantime we have cut building
steadily, to public services that the brighter,
more secure have no need for. In the future
you may need them, but the future is a

notion, distant and unknowable, it is a
distraction. What we are promising is more.
What we promise is a secure future
and this will be true, for some. More secure
as the great sun of the City shines brighter,
casts its shadow. Look what we are building.

This is our future. What we have is a
mandate to fulfil, building a Britain more
secure. And for us, it will be brighter.

Sunday

The rain lashes down like a TV's static
as smokers huddle under pubs' lintels –
from the Lescar across to Porter Cottage
the storm turns from drizzle to dismal.
Bless he who, with the cool persistence
of a craftsman, re-rolls a soggy Rizla;
opening the botched attempt in silence
as he rolls it into another.

When you leave with her, the sky has cleared:
a van trundles down Sharrowvale past
the shell of a butcher's, boarded and barred;
the sun and bulky nimbus in weird contrast
as you open up the Marlboros, offer her one,
struggling to recall if it was accident or arson.

Byroads

(i)

Hanging baskets frosted white
in the orange blur of a maple wood dusk,
ice stalactites rigid towards the pavements.

The firing of some gun from the wood's
clearing. A bus rumbles on, coughing,
and a local makes his turn at the pub's carpark.

(ii)

The village shop's newsboard
bears pictures of twenty-somethings
last seen by a farmer, a dog walker,

fourish on the forest's edge: a thick fog lingering,
spores shrouding the milling groups of deer. Ahead,
the brook flows near to where the search ended.

(iii)

Ploughed into the limestone wall
of a roadside house, the yellow
Beetle's bonnet kinks sharply out,

torn; the police at the kerbside directing
traffic and taking statements. The borderline
where post boxes change from red to green.

(iv)

Hillside housing estates flicker with lights,
windows shut against the winter's cold.
The backfields fold between them

and a stretched A-road; ice, potholes, nettled bushes,
a makeshift sign saying 'No Golf'. Grass peters out
to bracken, cat's eyes blink through the foliage.

Stag

The one I saw on the bypass that night –
antlers like a winter oak
as it strode from the roadside –
came again in a dream; keeping
its distance as it does every time.

When I met it for real I kept mine:
a stalled presence
on a stretch without streetlights;
its silhouette held there
before it turned and left.

In the dream, though, I follow –
into fields and meadows
where it spots me, begins to trot,
picks up pace before bolting off.
What if I could get close enough,

look it in those cavernous eyes?
What else could I hope to find
but yours, as all you said
echoes in my mind,
its glare passing through me?

Rooms

That amber light colouring the walls
   as we took the stairs up one by one,
leaving the last sparks of the fire
   to sink into embers and dark.

If I'd turned back then, I could think on
   that room's evidence: pore over
a guitar's silent moan, fag butts
   and empties – its version of events.

As if it might lend the clues that,
   pieced into some sort of sense,
would make our later rush
   seem selfish, or strangely selfless.

Let's say it was both. Funny how you
   can find yourself lost in the world,
lost in another's arms, like finding out
   all you thought you knew was wrong.

There are mornings I wake
   not to alarms or the radio's talk,
but with the dream of that room
   which, for a moment, still rings true.

The Argument

                    still stews in the hearts of these two –
a flaw in the foundations of the tall terraced house
they moved to six months back: this lass who, just now,
is sat upstairs on a bed, coaxing notes from a clarinet

as her guy props the tent of Frost's *A Witness Tree*
on the breakfast bar, looks at the yard, flicks the kettle on.
A cold winter: their first under the same roof. The sun
skim-reads them through separate windows.

And it isn't that they won't come through this, but what
the house alone, insidious, is able to articulate. Half-empty
cups on a table. A dust-thick windowsill. A washer spinning
through its final cycle, like a HGV thundering downhill.

The Leash

Snow ploughed up high on the pavements
and snow still drifting down,
us, wandering back from Rivelin at dusk
tired, slipping in bad shoes
and wrapped in long winter coats,

remember bumping into that drunk
and his flea-bitten dog?
I felt for that Staffie, all bloodshot eyes
and bark worse than its bite,
even as it sniffed out my fear

to start snapping at my side.
We laughed about it afterwards –
me skittering on ice as it leapt around –
but I swear its look of anger was
sadness, leashed tight to the here and now.

Marine

after Paul Verlaine

This sea's tumbling waters
ebb and flow, beat below
the moon's sorrowful stare,
beat again and again.

Dark clouds are drifting in.
Sudden and sinister,
a lightning bolt fissures
the sky's murky bistre.

Over the beach and rocks
waves come and fall apart.
Now the seagulls start up
shouting, or else crying.

Look into the distance.
A boat's hazy outline
is that thought at the edge
of your mind. Wait for it.

Two Clouds

Think of mornings we'd head for the hills,
the world quiet for the chatter of water,
a lone walker calling back his dog, still
deep in the woods' deepening shelter.
The rain would pelt us like pine needles:
us, struggling up Clough Lane again,
making sense of the sky's doodles,
chance and happenstance and change.

I ran those paths alone today, pausing
at the forge's broken waterwheel,
the faint sound of a distant barking
ringing the valley to sharpened steel.
Clear skies, like only in winter. Yet I swear
two clouds mapped the hillside together.

Songs

after Marina Tsvetaeva

Where did our tenderness come from?
As if yours were the first curls
I'd felt close, ran fingers through.
You've kissed lips darker than mine.

The night came cold and starless,
snowstorms swept in from the east.
Though others' eyes have met mine
with that same, uncertain peace.

But I've never known songs like these,
songs that still go on ... the dark
pulled close, my head on your chest,
and the world clear-cut for once.

Where did our tenderness come from?
What to make of it? Love,
I imagine you passing me by –
your azure eyes, sharper than anyone's.

Above Stanage

When else but that day we were caught on the ridge
   in a storm so fierce in its sudden grip
      fields moved like water?

     And how the wind
   tore a path there before us;
the landscape loosened from its guy ropes.

Farcical, like something out of a Brontë novel,
   with that touch of the realistic absurd –
      our umbrella flung inside out

     and you hardly uttering a word...
Here again, I struggle to turn it back on itself.
As if I'm not soaked already. As if we might work things out.

Bearing

Watching him that spring-spilled-into-summer,
sat among Algar Seco's jagged rocks,

steadfast with rod, tub of bait,
water, hunk of bread,

still as a stork in its nest
settled above the walls of Silves,

I recovered what it was to wait –
content, not out of hope or faith

but for the catch that always comes;
a clutch of silver by dusk

like us, stumbling onto the beach one night,
finding that added depth in each other's eyes.

The Door

What was it that brought us out that day
from pints and talk, our corner snug,
down streets still slick with rain?

A mist had thickened to clinging fog –
the road deserted except distant traffic,
blinking away like lifeboats at sea.

Forgetting ourselves, it seemed a trick
when the city gave way to fields, empty
as all we weren't saying, but thinking.

I'm thinking now of that barn we saw.
Dilapidated, abandoned; sparrows darting
from its roof; but most of all the door

where no door was, bricked up
yet suddenly revealing itself,
like a portal between worlds.

Let's say it was. Let's say all we felt
stood there, all we've held off. Let's walk
through that door, love, and never look back.

A Prayer

See the hot coals in my eyes,
these sparks where I walk?
I want to be lost
for the rest of my life;

to wander like a fox
led by the moment's promise,
whistling as I stumble
through empty meadows.

I want to kip in the woods,
read the sky's story
instead of old books,
greet the day as a skimmed stone

and know the rainfall
as I'll know the soles of my feet.
I want to leap into the river
and feel each day's heat,

to run along path after path
as if endlessly confined;
to sweep through my life restlessly,
slowly clearing a place to die.

Notes

'To David Foster Wallace' – the American novelist, short story writer and essayist (1962–2008).

'Sundays too my Dad got up early' – from a line in Robert Hayden's 'Those Winter Sundays'.

'Where I Run From' – the first line of the poem is the title of a memoir by the Japanese novelist Haruki Murakami, in which he writes of his interest and participation in long-distance running.

'Kenny Dalglish' – refers to Sunday 16 April 1989, the day after the disaster at the Hillsborough Stadium in Sheffield, England, where 96 Liverpool fans lost their lives.

'Bruce Grobbelaar' – makes reference to the Liverpool goalkeeper's alleged involvement in match-fixing. It also refers to his famous technique of 'spaghetti legs' and other off-putting goal-line tactics.

'Steven Gerrard' – on the morning of 27 April 2014, Liverpool were three wins from lifting their first league title in 24 years. The then-captain Steven Gerrard slipped while receiving a pass during a match versus Chelsea at Anfield. This allowed Chelsea to open the scoring, who went on to win the game 2-0. Liverpool would finish the season in second place; Gerrard later referred to the period as 'the worst three months of my life'.

'Luis Suárez' – refers to a game at Anfield on 21 April 2013, during which Suárez bit the Chelsea defender Branislav Ivanović. It also refers to an alleged incident from the player's youth, in which he apparently headbutted a referee.

'John Barnes' – on 10 June 1984, while playing for England, Barnes scored a goal against Brazil. It brought him instant fame, though it did little to silence the racism he experienced throughout his career as a black player.

Acknowledgements

Thanks to the editors of the following publications, where many of these poems first appeared: *The Bolton Review, Edinburgh Review, The Guardian, Liverpool FC Monthly, METER: the runner's review, Millstone Grit, The Morning Star, New Boots and Pantisocracies* (Smokestack Books, 2015), *New Welsh Review, The North, One for the Road: an anthology of pubs and poetry* (smith/doorstop, 2017), *Poetry London, Poetry Review, Poetry Spotlight, The Rialto, The Salt Book of Younger Poets, The Sheffield Anthology* (smith/doorstop, 2012), *The Spectator, Times Literary Supplement, Wordlife: an anthology* (Opus Independents, 2016). Some of these poems also appeared in my pamphlets *The Sparks* (tall-lighthouse, 2008) and *For Real* (smith/doorstop, 2014). 'John Barnes' won first prize in the *Offside Stories: The Pride and the Passion* competition, judged by Ian McMillan.

I'm grateful to the Northern Writers' Awards for gifting me the Northern Promise Award, and to both Arts Council England and the University of Bolton for support that enabled the completion of many of these poems.

Many thanks go to all who have variously helped with advice, particularly in editing and shaping these poems on their long journey to book publication: Alan Buckley, Alan Malpass, Amy Wack, Andrew Jamison, Bev Nadin, Conor O'Callaghan, Ellen McLeod, Helen Mort, John Challis, John McCullough, Maurice Riordan, Niall Campbell, Peter Sansom.

This book is dedicated to my parents and family, for their unfailing support and belief.